Painting on Porcelain

The author would like to thank the museum curators and European collectors who have made it possible for her to revive the patterns of period pieces of porcelain and earthenware, and her husband Claude, who has helped and encouraged her, and also photographed the porcelain and earthenware.

Annick Perret

Painting on Porcelain

traditional and contemporary designs

Translated by Malcolm Withell

SEARCH PRESS

First published in Great Britain 1993
Search Press Limited
Wellwood, North Farm Road,
Tunbridge Wells, Kent TN2 3DR

Reprinted 2000

This book has been rewritten and rearranged from
illustrations and material from *Oiseaux et Bouquets: Peinture
sur Porcelaine* and *Peinture sur Porcelaine: Décors
Traditionelles et Contemporains,* both by Annick Perret,
published in French by Dessain et Tolra, Paris: copyright ©
respectively 1991 and 1992 Dessain et Tolra.

The Publishers would like to thank Ms Gigi Branch, who
kindly advised us on the technical terms and procedures used
in this book.

There are references to sable and other animal-hair brushes
in this book. It is the Publishers' custom to recommend
synthetic materials as substitutes for animal products
wherever possible. There are now many brushes available
made of artificial fibres and these are as satisfactory as
brushes made of natural fibres.

ISBN 0 85532 766 9

Printed in Spain by A.G. Elkar S. Coop, 48012 Bilbao.

Contents

Introduction

Painting on porcelain is an art form which has always fascinated me. There really are so many possibilities, from plates and teapots to trinket-boxes and sweet-dishes, and over the twenty-five years I have been painting on porcelain I have probably tried most of them!

I also decided to make a special study of porcelain plaques, so as not to be tied to the shape of an object. These plaques are generally small and modern, set off by a carefully chosen border in a complementary colour.

The birds and floral paintings are inspired by antique porcelain and earthenware. These patterns have been interpreted and painted in watercolours after studies made when visiting various European museums. They will help painters – beginners or advanced – to get acquainted with the technique of relief and shading of birds and flowers.

Although many of my patterns have been inspired by antique pieces in museums and private collections, others are entirely the product of my imagination. Inspiration comes from all quarters: people, nature, letters of the alphabet, early artists…and simply out of my own head. So my designs range from the strictly traditional to the contemporary and abstract – something for every taste.

I hope the ideas in this book inspire you: the designs can be painted not only on porcelain but also on earthenware, wood, silk, fabric, or whatever surface your imagination may suggest.

Annick Perret

Publishers' note

Ready-prepared paints

In this book the author has concentrated on the classic method of preparing colours, but you will find that there are also pre-prepared, ready-to-use paints available, which are sold in a compressed 'pastille' form and can be used rather like watercolours, using a mixture of half water and half alcohol as a solvent. Most of these colours can be mixed, except for the reds, pinks and oranges, and you will find that these paints dry quickly.

You can also find porcelain paints in paste form, sold in pots, like gouache.

If, however, you are interested in creating purely decorative objects which will not be used as tableware or be subjected to heat, there are now other options available.

Cold ceramic paints, for example, come in liquid form, in a wide range of colours which can be mixed with one another. They require no special preparation or firing, and can be mixed with a colourless medium to increase their transparency. Glossy and durable, they dry in around three hours. They are, however, not heat-resistant and should not be used on anything which is to come into contact with food.

You can also get some lovely effects with transparent glass paints, or enamel paints.

Please follow the manufacturers' instructions in all cases.

Materials, equipment and techniques

Porcelain

This book deals with the technique of on-glaze painting. You should therefore buy plain white glazed porcelain for decorating. (Clean it with alcohol to ensure it is completely grease-free before you start painting on it, and be careful not to get greasy fingermarks on it while you are working.)

There are all sorts of different styles and shapes available. Obviously the decoration on an object must fit in with its shape! For example, you could not paint a contemporary design on a traditional *rocaille* teapot; on the other hand the shape of a modern teapot (such as 'Caspar, Melchior and Balthasar', on page 78) lends itself more to fantasy.

You can paint on ornamental objects (this is the classic style), or on porcelain and earthenware plaques to be displayed on the wall.

Brushes

Choose very good quality paintbrushes (brushes especially for painting on porcelain). These should be of pure sable or squirrel hair. I use the following brushes (numbered from left to right in the picture).

Stippler brushes (1)

These are for filling in small areas. They are slightly bevelled, or straight, and you will need several different sizes of them.

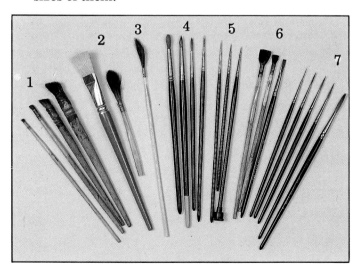

A selection of brushes for painting on porcelain.

Brushes for colouring in (2)

You will need these for filling in backgrounds. They are brushes with long, soft hairs; you can also use brushes of the fish-tail type.

Cut liners (3)

These have long, sloping hairs, and are used for lining or banding with the aid of a turntable. Keep some brushes for precious metals and some for colours; you should never use the same brush for both colours and gold.

Pointers (4)

These are for general painting, shading and shadowing. You will need several sizes of these brushes.

Brushes for outlining (5)

Very fine brushes are required for outlining and shading flowers and the feathers of birds. You will need three sizes: Nos. 00, 0, and 1.

Square shaders (6)

You will need these for painting larger areas and for certain contemporary patterns.

Long pointers (7)

These brushes, with their long, pointed hairs, are for detail work and for scrolling. (I particularly like using these). You will need five sizes. Everyone has his own preferences for particular brushes; just try them out and choose those that suit your own style of work.

Cleaning brushes

I clean my brushes with turpentine essence, and I impregnate the hairs with an oil which stops them going hard (carnation oil, for example). If the hairs on a brush get too hard, I just soften them up slowly in turpentine. Brushes last a long time if they are used and maintained carefully. It is better not to clean them in methylated spirit, as there is a risk of spoiling the hairs.

Other equipment

Agate burnisher

This is a small piece of agate mounted on a handle, used for burnishing gold.

Carnation oil

This prolongs the time a prepared colour is workable (it dries less quickly than oils of spike lavender, aspic, cloves, etc.).

Dividers

These will help you divide up a plate, cup, etc., into equal parts.

Fat oil

Fat oil is thickened turpentine essence which is used for preparing colours. There is one available which dries very slowly, just right for certain patterns.

Fibreglass brush

This is a special glass or fibreglass brush for polishing gold.

Glass containers or jam-jars

You will need these for putting turpentine in, cleaning brushes and preparing colours, and to put gold in.

Glass rod

This is for stirring the gold before use and for stopping it settling at the bottom of the bottle.

Gold

This precious metal comes as a liquid solution. Bright gold contains about 12 per cent gold, and shines after firing; you can get some interesting effects using it in certain patterns. When I make gilded pieces (cup handles, for example), I apply a coat of bright gold, fire it, and then recoat with matt 32 per cent gold, which I burnish after the second firing.

Matt or burnishing gold, as its name suggests, stays matt after firing. You can buy it as 24 per cent or 32 per cent gold. It must be polished with agate, or polishing sand, or a fibreglass brush. I always use 32 per cent fine gold on my porcelain.

Gold eraser

This is used for rubbing off mistakes on the gold after firing.

Gold thinners

Use these for cleaning brushes which you have used for gold, and for diluting gold which is too thick.

Graphite paper

Use special graphite paper for slipping under tracing paper to reproduce your drawing on to the porcelain.

Kiln

Ceramic kilns for amateur use are becoming increasingly easy to find at specialist outlets, and they are very easy to use for firing your patterns.

Medium

This is a ready-prepared mix of fat oil with other oils (it replaces the traditional mixture).

Methylated spirit

You can use this for cleaning and degreasing porcelain and certain brushes used for lustre finishes, but it is better to use special lustre thinners for the latter.

Palette

You can get these with porcelain bowls (the lid of the palette is used for preparing the colours, and the bowls are to put the colours or prepared mixes in).

You can also use white earthenware tiles for preparing colours and trying them out.

Palette knives

These, which are essential, consist of a flexible steel blade mounted on a wooden handle, and are used for colour preparation (for grinding the paint granules).

Pencil

Buy a special lithographic pencil, which is like a wax crayon made for drawing on porcelain or earthenware. The lines it makes will vanish completely after firing.

Platinum

This precious metal, when matt, is worked and polished like burnishing gold (after firing). Bright platinum comes out of the kiln in a burnished state.

Scraper

Use this, or a rubbing-out knife, or toothpicks, for scraping colour off the porcelain or correcting details.

Synthetic foam pad

You will need one for padding large areas of colour.

Thinners

These are for thinning precious metals.

Tracing paper

Tracing paper is used for transferring drawings to the porcelain.

Turntable

Also known as a banding wheel or whirler, this is a circular revolving platform on which you centre your piece of porcelain to paint bands (fillets) or thin lines round it, using gold or a colour. Hold your brush with a steady hand and touch the piece lightly with the brush while the turntable is going round – you will find, with practice, that the band will turn out absolutely regular.

Turpentine essence

Used for the preparation of colours according to traditional and classic formulae, this is obtained by distilling conifer resin.

Vitrifying colours

These are on-glaze enamels, firing at temperatures between 680 and 820°C (1256 and 1508°F). (I use powdered colours of various makes).

Colours

You will find powder colours (on-glaze colours) of various makes. These, which are vitrifiable colours specially formulated for working on glazed porcelain or earthenware (firing between 680 and 820°C (1256 and 1508°F)), are metal oxide colourings which when mixed with flux adhere to the porcelain glaze.

N.B. You can also buy ready-made porcelain paints – see the Introduction for more about them.

Preparing the colours

I myself prepare colours using the classic method, following the traditional formula.

Put some colour powder on the earthenware tile, mix it to a smooth, non-grainy paste with a very small amount of rectified turpentine essence, add fat oil, and then one or two drops of carnation oil or oil of spike lavender (to stop the mixture drying too quickly). Work the mixture well with the palette knife.

First stage

Apply the paint to the porcelain in thin transparent coats, then carry out the first firing.

Second stage

Continue working, accentuating the shading, depth of colours, etc. Fire a second time and, if necessary, a third time if touching up needs to be done. It is best to do several firings when you are doing complicated work on porcelain.

Experimenting with colour

Porcelain colours nearly always alter in shade after firing, so in order to familiarise yourself with colours, I advise mixing up a palette of colours on a porcelain plate. Try painting three shades of the same colours – light, medium and dark – so that you can take note of the difference after firing. Write the number or name of each colour against each example, and keep this plate as a firing reference.

Every make has its own colours with its own numbers or names. For example, apple green or emerald green of one make will be different from those of another make. This chart of a few base colours (painted in watercolours) is a close match with the colours I use for painting on porcelain. It should be done on a plate and fired at about 800°C (1472°F).

With one colour, three different shades can be obtained.

Light: one coat of the colour.

Medium: two coats of the colour (intermediate firing).

Dark: three coats of the colour (intermediate firings).

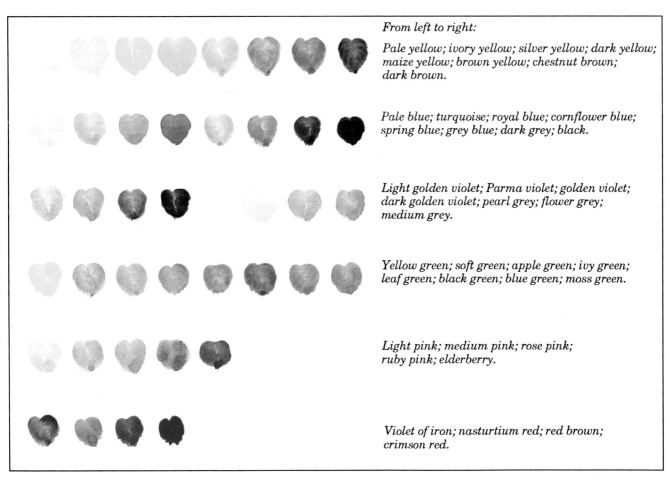

From left to right:

Pale yellow; ivory yellow; silver yellow; dark yellow; maize yellow; brown yellow; chestnut brown; dark brown.

Pale blue; turquoise; royal blue; cornflower blue; spring blue; grey blue; dark grey; black.

Light golden violet; Parma violet; golden violet; dark golden violet; pearl grey; flower grey; medium grey.

Yellow green; soft green; apple green; ivy green; leaf green; black green; blue green; moss green.

Light pink; medium pink; rose pink; ruby pink; elderberry.

Violet of iron; nasturtium red; red brown; crimson red.

The darker the colour you wish to paint, the more you have to repeat the process of another coat of colour and an intermediate firing.

Colour superimposition using six colours

First firing: divide up the earthenware tile into six vertical bands. Take yellow, iron red or nasturtium red, rose pink, olive green or ivy green, turquoise blue, otter brown, or chestnut brown, and apply them in vertical bands with a broad brush without pressing hard. Fire at 740°C (1364°F).

Second firing: now apply the same colours, in the same order, this time painting them in horizontal bands (yellow, red, rose pink, green, blue, brown). Fire at 740°C (1364°F).

Colour superimposition chart painted on a tile.

2 coats of yellow	red on yellow	rose pink on yellow	green on yellow	blue on yellow	brown on yellow
1 coat yellow	red	rose pink	green	blue	brown
yellow on red	2 coats of nasturtium red	rose pink on red	green on red	blue on red	brown on red
1 coat yellow	red	rose pink	green	blue	brown
yellow on rose pink	red on rose pink	2 coats of rose pink	green on rose pink	blue on rose pink	brown on rose pink
1 coat yellow	red	rose pink	green	blue	brown
yellow on green	red on green	rose pink on green	2 coats of green	blue on green	brown on green
1 coat yellow	red	rose pink	green	blue	brown
yellow on blue	red on blue	rose pink on blue	green on blue	2 coats of blue	brown on blue
1 coat yellow	red	rose pink	green	blue	brown
yellow on brown	red on brown	rose pink on brown	green on brown	blue on brown	2 coats of brown

A test chart painted on a tile to try out the effect of using colours with grey.

From left to right:

Grey; golden violet + 75% grey; golden violet + 50% grey; golden violet + 25% grey; golden violet.

Grey; blue + 75% grey; blue + 50% grey; blue + 25% grey; cornflower blue.

Grey; red + 75% grey; red + 50% grey; red + 25% grey; nasturtium red.

Grey; yellow + 75% grey; yellow + 50% grey; yellow + 25% grey; silver yellow

Grey; green + 75% grey; green + 50% grey; green + 25% grey; apple green.

This exercise can be performed with other colours, in order to perfect your technique and find out for yourself the results of the superimpositions – do it on porcelain with a firing temperature of 800 to 820°C (1442 to 1508°F). I very often use pinks (which have a gold base) in my mixes or superimpositions to enhance certain colours or pick them out.

Trying out new colours with grey *(see opposite)*

Only one firing is required for this.

Divide the plaque up into twenty-five squares. Take dark golden violet, cornflower blue, nasturtium red, silver yellow, apple green, medium grey. In each square on the extreme right, apply the pure colours (golden violet, blue, etc.). In each of the squares on the left, apply medium grey. Then mix each colour with the grey: for example, golden violet with 75% grey, golden violet with 50% grey, golden violet with 25% grey. Do the same with the other colours and apply them in the appropriate square. Fire at 740°C (1364°F). Make other test palettes by mixing the colours; this will show you the results after firing, and is very instructive.

As you can see, with the light or medium grey which I have mixed with apple green, yellow, nasturtium red, cornflower blue and dark golden violet I have achieved a palette of fifteen lovely new separate nuances of colour. Fire it at around 740°C (1364°F).

Even an experienced painter is always making new discoveries. It is vital to master the art of colour if you wish to launch into producing your own designs. By mixing or superimposing colours, you will very quickly achieve a personal touch with tones of colour. Experimenting is very important!

Techniques

Technique of firing

Firing the design is not at all difficult, but if you do not have an electric kiln with a muffle allowing the firing of colours on porcelain, you will find specialist shops that will be able to give you recommendations or will do the firing themselves for you.

Firing for on-glaze painting should be done in an electric ceramic kiln: about 780°C (1256°F) for earthenware, with a slow increase in temperature up to 720°C (1298°F), and about 800°C (1472°F) for porcelain, with a rapid increase in temperature and keeping it at 800°C (1472°F) for fifteen minutes.

Soft firing is done with a brush on glazed surfaces with vitrifiable colours which are transformed by fusion in an electric oven and take on a lustrous, solid look when they have cooled.

Superimposing several coats of the same colour gives it an ever-increasing intensity; one firing must be made for each coat of colour. If the coat is too thick, the porcelain glaze will not be able to absorb it, and it will peel off or chip.

My designs need several coats with successive firings. It is the heat which gives porcelain its lasting solidity and lustre. However, firing can also destroy everything! This is where experience will make all the difference.

Porcelain plaques often require from four to six firings. Colours are finished off with lustres which, after firing, give iridescence and brilliance to the colours. Precious metals are also used: burnishing gold (32 per cent pure), bright gold, matt platinum and bronze.

The technique of successive firings allows effects which enhance the iridescence of the piece. It is a constant struggle, though, and you always have to be on the watch because the next firing could destroy everything!

Other techniques

Brushing

This means spreading the colour evenly and brushing, padding and evening it out with a small stippler brush (for small areas) or a foam pad (for large areas). Clean the foam pad by soaking it in turpentine, and then wash it with lukewarm water and ordinary household soap and leave it to dry in a fine linen cloth away from dust.

Burnishing with agate

If you burnish matt/burnishing gold with an agate tool you can get brilliant effects (matt-brilliant) – see the example of the decorated eggs.

Drawing with a pen

This means using a strong steel-nibbed pen to draw very thin lines. You will need to prepare the paint so that it flows easily off your nib, and you should load your pen very lightly and keep wiping it to stop it clogging up.

Gold firing

For porcelain, on a colour background, fire at about 680°C (1256°F); and on white porcelain at about 800°C (1472°F).

Imitation etching

Using this special yellowy paste, make a garland of this colour on the porcelain, then, after firing, cover the border with burnishing gold. After the second firing, polish the gold. The garland will have more of a matt finish than the background.

Iridisation of colours

After painting iridescent lustre on the porcelain, fire, and then paint a pale colour on to the lustre. Fire a second time.

Marbling

To get this effect, put on (using a brush or a pad) a background of irregular colour, using two shades (light and dark) to give a mottled or veined effect.

Masking fluid

Use this special fluid for protecting an area which has to remain white: paint the fluid on to the area you wish to remain white and let it dry. Then paint the background colour over the whole area, let the paint dry, and remove the masking fluid, which will come off easily (you must not forget to do this before firing!).

Polishing or burnishing gold

Rub gold with special fine polishing sand or a special fibreglass brush. This will give matt or burnishing gold a fine appearance.

Pouncing

You can use a pouncing pattern for repeating a drawing: first draw the design on tracing paper and prick the outline with a needle, making small, regular holes. Then turn the paper over and rub it over gently with very fine glasspaper (to open out the holes). Rub the pouncer (a cloth pad containing or impregnated with pounce (powdered charcoal)) across the tracing in swirls, and you will find that the charcoal marks out the outline.

Preparing colour with oil

The oil keeps the colour fresh longer (it dries more slowly than with a turpentine preparation). It is very useful for doing thin lines and working with a pen, using a mixture of oil and fat oil.

Relief

You can get some interesting effects using white relief paste, which can be coloured (be careful, though: relief is tricky to use as it chips very easily). It is sold as a white powder, which you pulverise with a knife and some terpineol (light pine oil) and make into a paste. It is applied with a brush. To make a gilded relief, put relief paste specially formulated for gold on the porcelain and coat with burnishing gold after firing.

Scraping the painting

Scraping the colour when dry with a sharp-pointed piece of wood or a scraper/rubbing-out knife can produce some interesting and attractive designs.

Speckling

For this effect, put on colour almost dry (with very little turpentine) with a foam pad. You can also use a toothbrush if you keep the colour a bit more liquid.

Threading

The term means thin lines painted on the porcelain by using a turntable. Fine or broad lines can be drawn using colours or precious metals.

Using lustres

These are metallic salts used as colorants, sold in specialist shops together with a crackling solution, and they give superb effects after firing. (You can also get lustres already mixed with the solution). I suggest you make up a sample plate so that you get acquainted with lustres, which all look brown before firing.

Paint on pure lustre and, to lighten it, add a little special lustre-thinner. Clean the brushes (kept specially for working with lustres) with lustre-thinners or (in an emergency) methylated spirits. Generally, lustres can be mixed with each other, but there are one or two that cannot, so be careful when you test them out!

Mother-of-pearl lustre is really superb – try using it on butterflies' wings to give them a lovely iridescent effect.

Lustres can be applied with a foam pad to achieve a uniform surface. You must cut off the end of the pad afterwards, though, as it cannot be cleaned up.

You should fire lustres for earthenware at 680 to 700°C (1256 to 1292°F) and for porcelain at 780 to 800°C (1436 to 1472°F). If you put gold on a lustre background, fire at 800°C (1472°F). When I put gold on a lustre background, I burnish it with agate.

Using bronze

Bronze is used in the same way as lustre.

How to start

Before putting the patterns on to the porcelain itself, I always project my thoughts on to paper and try out a range of colours, developing the subject as I see the result of each firing. The different stages of my work are as follows.

On paper: preliminary thoughts, leading to a drawing of the finished article; test palette; mixture of colours; trying out patterns, etc.

On the piece of porcelain: actually on the porcelain plaque, plate, medallion, or whatever.

I reproduce my design on the porcelain with tracing paper. After going over it with ink or a very fine brush to mark the outlines, I go on to the colours and the intermediate firings. I always keep a mental picture of the finished piece while I am working on it.

Flowers and leaves

Flower studies

To sketch the violets, morning glory and tulip, study the directions of the arrows in the picture on page 15 and follow them with your brush-strokes.

Violets
Sketch the petals with light gold violet, royal blue and silver yellow, with a touch of bronze brown, then shade them with dark gold violet, dark cornflower blue, sepia brown and dark brown (for the yellow petals). Sketch the leaves with moss green and brown green, and shade them with violet of iron and black green.

Morning glory
Sketch the morning glories with royal blue mixed with a little light pink, silver yellow and bronze brown. Then shade them with cornflower blue. The leaves are painted in moss green and olive green.

Tulip bouquet
Sketch the tulip with light pink and medium pink, and blend in some silver yellow as shown in the picture. Shade the tulip with elderberry. The leaves are painted in apple green and emerald green. The little flower above the tulip (see page 16) is painted with rose pink mixed with medium blue, silver yellow, violet of iron, and a mixture of black and green.

*First firing: sketch the tulip with medium pink
and blend in some silver yellow.*

First firing: sketch the morning glory and the violets.

The finished flowers.

Pink flower plate

Two firings.
Painted on porcelain (fired at 780 to 800°C (1436 to 1472°F)).

Paint a celadon background on the rim of the plate. After the first firing, set it off with a garland of foliage in moss green mixed with celadon green, then fire it for a second time.

First firing: sketching.

Second firing: shading.

Bouquet 1

The following colours are used: medium pink, dark rose pink, golden yellow, sepia, royal blue, cornflower blue, fir-tree green, violet of iron, black green.

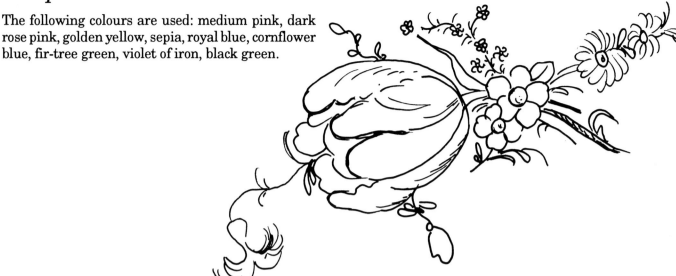

Bouquet 2

The following colours are used: medium pink, dark rose pink, royal blue, cornflower blue, golden yellow, sepia, fir-tree green, violet of iron, black green.

You can shade the three little yellow roses with a mixture of violet of iron and black green.

Bouquet 3

The following colours are used: medium pink, dark rose pink, royal blue with a touch of maroon, dark golden violet, pearl grey, skyline grey, fir-tree green, violet of iron, black green.

Shade the royal blue mixed with a touch of maroon with dark golden violet, and the fir-tree green with violet of iron and black green.

Tulips, roses and narcissi

The following colours are used:

Narcissi: silver grey, dark grey, silver yellow, nasturtium red, green.

Roses: medium pink, maroon.

Blue flowers: royal blue, cornflower blue, silver yellow, maroon.

Sprays of little flowers: nasturtium red, with a dot of black green.

Tulip: medium pink, maroon, silver yellow, sepia.

Leaves: soft green, moss green, meadow green, emerald green, violet of iron, black green.

First firing: sketch the bouquet, following the direction of the brush strokes shown for the tulip and the rose (see the little arrows).

Second firing: now shade each flower with stronger colours. Shade the foliage with elderberry and green, or violet of iron and black green.

Sketching the tulip with rose pink, silver yellow, sepia. First firing.

Shading the tulip with dark rose pink and sepia. Second firing.

Rose bouquet

The following colours are used: light gold violet, dark gold violet, royal blue, cornflower blue, silver yellow, black green, medium pink, Dresden dark rose pink, meadow green, soft green, emerald green, sepia.

Sketching the rose with rose pink. (Make sure you follow the direction of the arrows.)

Shading with dark rose pink.

The finished bouquet.

The finished bouquet.

21

Peony bouquet

The following colours are used: light pink, medium pink, dark rose pink, pale coral red, dark coral red, golden yellow, chestnut brown, royal blue, cornflower blue, dark golden violet, lilac, violet of iron, pearl grey, skyline grey, dark grey, black green; and for the foliage use fir-tree green, black green, emerald green, Veronese green, Russian green.

First firing: sketch each flower, following the direction of the brush-strokes for the petals. For the peony, use medium pink and elderberry; its centre is golden

yellow, with a touch of ivory yellow and a bit of chestnut brown. Paint the little rose in pale coral red.

Second firing: go over each flower again, giving them as much bulk as possible. Paint the peony petals in elderberry and shade them with fine cross-hatched lines. Shade the centre with chestnut brown or a mixture of violet of iron and black green, and the little rose with dark coral red. Finally shade the foliage with black green, and emerald green mixed with elderberry.

The finished bouquet.

Roses and forget-me-nots

The following colours are used: light pink, dark rose pink, golden yellow, pearl grey, skyline grey, light golden violet (or a mixture of lilac and rose pink); for the foliage use Veronese green, fir-tree green, emerald green, brown.

Shading the foliage with brown and green.

24

Tulip bouquet

Two firings.

Painted on earthenware
(fired at 680 to 720°C (1256
to 1298°F).

The finishing touch is the
elderberry line on the rim
of the dish.

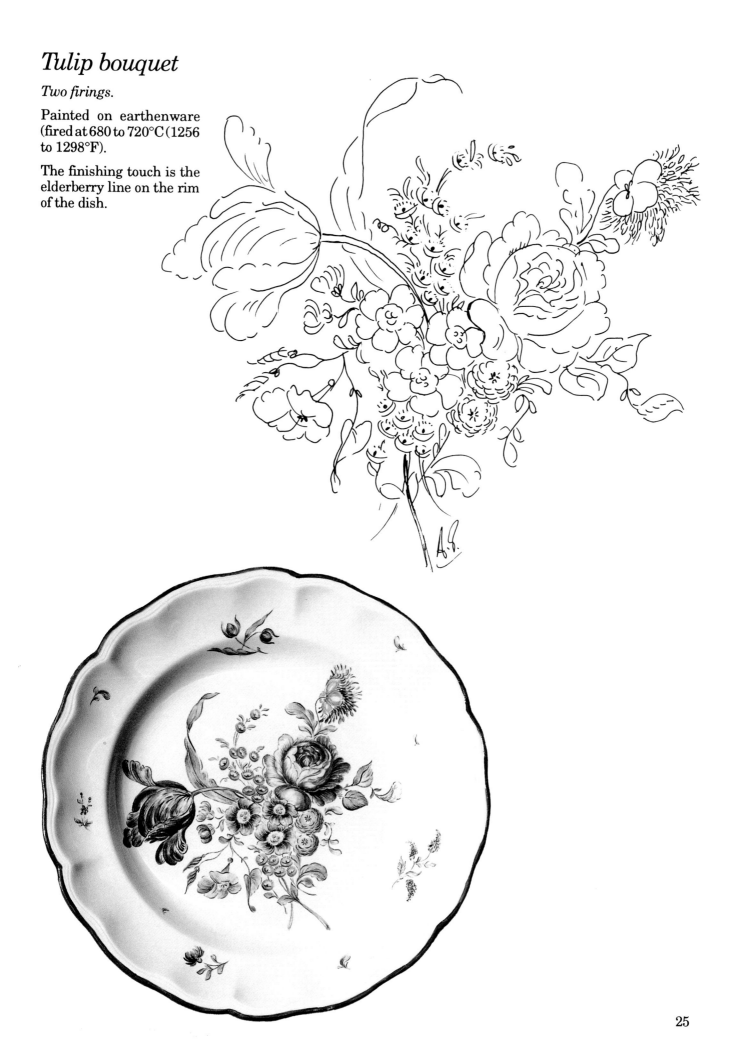

Oval dish with pink flowers

Two firings.

Painted on earthenware (fired at 680 to 720°C (1256 to 1298°F)).

Finish off by painting a maroon line on the rim of the oval dish.

To create the plate pictured on page 1, follow the same procedure, but paint the border in elderberry.

Mixed bouquet

The following colours are used: rose pink, ruby purple, lilac mixed with rose pink, dark golden violet, golden yellow, orange yellow, clove brown, royal blue, cornflower blue; for the foliage use Empire green, emerald green, soft green, black green, violet of iron.

Shade the lilac mixed with rose pink, using dark golden violet.

Flower plate

Two firings.

Painted on earthenware (fired at 680 to 720°C (1256 to 1298°F)).

The finishing touch is a border painted in elderberry.

Pansies

Three firings.

Painted on porcelain (fired at 780 to 800°C (1436 to 1472°F)).

I made a collection of white porcelain eggs from Limoges and decorated them myself. Some of the designs have been inspired by reproductions or old postcards, but most of them are my own design.

For this egg, first sketch and shade the flowers; then paint a light graduated background in apple green and yellow. Finish off by painting the feet and border of the egg emerald green.

Wild roses and insects

Three firings.

Sketch the wild roses and fill them in lightly with light pink, light yellow, and a touch of pale blue. Then shade the contours of the petals with medium pink.

Paint the centres of the flowers with violet of iron, a little black green, and yellow. Then fill in the background evenly with pale apple green and pale yellow, protecting the bouquet and the insects with masking fluid.

Daffodils and daisies

Four firings.

First firing: a broad line of iridescent lustre on the lid and the base of the egg.

Second firing: a garland of gold (painted with a fine brush) on the lustre (lid and base).

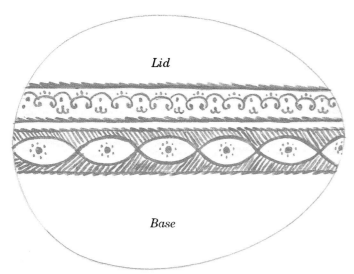

Sketch the bouquet and paint the daisies in base white (shade in lightly with soft green). The forget-me-nots are in pale-blue relief, outlined in dark blue. Paint the centres of the daisies with silver yellow and violet of iron, then the petals of the wild roses in rose pink and their centres in yellow, black green, and apple green.

For the daffodils, use light and dark yellow, celadon green, violet of iron, and a little black green.

After firing, the shading of the bouquet is done entirely with a pen; the foliage is in black green.

Orchid

Four firings.

First draw in the design with a pen or a small brush; put several brush strokes of grey lustre around the orchid; then sketch the orchid in golden violet.

For the third firing, put masking fluid on the orchid and the grey lustre to protect them, and make a mauve background with a bit of cornflower blue and rose pink, creating a slightly marbled effect with a foam pad.

For the fourth firing, work on the background in blue with a pen.

Mauve ribbon and garland

Four firings.

Divide the egg into three sections to design the ribbon and the garland; the floral garland will pass under the ribbon. The ribbon is painted in pale mauve, finished with 32 per cent burnishing gold. The three feet are all painted gold.

Orchid.

Mauve ribbon and garland.

Daisies on a coloured background

Two firings.

First firing: fill in the background of the egg in a very pale colour (blue, yellow, pink or green).

Second firing: shade the daisies in gold, and add small gold dots to the background.

Celadon-green ribbon with flowers

Four firings.

The following colours are used: spring blue, cornflower blue, soft green, celadon green, rose pink and 32 per cent gold.

The design is repeated three times round the egg.

On the lid, paint a little coronet of forget-me-nots, then fill in the ribbon using celadon green; finish off with small gold dots.

Shade in the forget-me-nots with spring blue and cornflower blue, and paint their centres pale yellow. The three feet of the base are done in burnishing gold.

Cornflowers and golden garland

Two firings.

For the design, divide into three equal parts; sketch the garland of cornflowers, the gold lines – a broad one and a fine one (made with the aid of a turntable) – and paint the gold lattice-work.

First firing: sketch the garland of cornflowers.

Second firing: shade in the garland and go over the gold. Note that the cornflowers are shaded at the tips (cornflower blue). The little dots are painted in elderberry.

Paint the foliage soft green, with shading in violet of iron and black green.

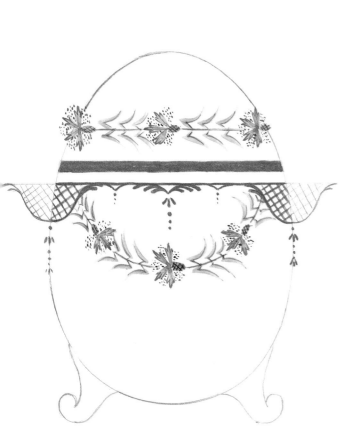

Poppies and ox-eye daisies

Three firings.

For the foliage, mix up a range of greens: soft green, apple green, emerald green and black green. The shading is done with a pen.

Paint the background of the base of the egg in Empire green, leaf green, or perhaps ivy green, and add a gold garland.

Paint the daisy petals in base white, and the centres in yellow and violet of iron. For the poppies, the petals should be nasturtium red, with black dots, and the centres black and emerald green.

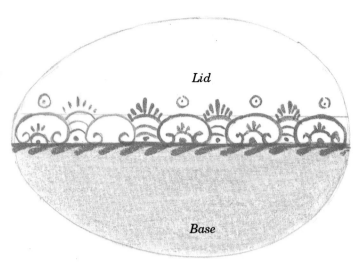

Leaves

Sweet chestnut leaf

Four firings.

Wing of the plate

The background is done in rust brown with a pebbled effect in matt platinum. The line, too, is matt platinum.

Bowl of the plate

The leaf is painted in pastel colours, with the aid of a turntable, and there are white reliefs and touches of matt platinum. I have outlined the leaf with rust brown.

Chestnut leaf

Five firings.

Use a turntable to make the circles on the chestnut leaf.

I have chosen very soft colours here: light brown ochre and rust brown for the background, with white reliefs.

Morning dew

Five firings.

I created this composition around two maple leaves.

The background is speckled, filled in with grey, yellow and green-blue. I have drawn patterns with a pen – gold dots and iridescent lustre.

The maple leaves are painted in white relief on a background of very pale yellow and blue.

Gold and black leaves

Three firings.

This is a free composition on an octagonal porcelain plate.

The following colours are used: black, maize, 32 per cent burnishing gold.

First firing: make the design; apply masking fluid to the motifs; fill in the plate in maize with a foam pad (heavier towards the centre). Remove the masking fluid before firing.

Second firing: paint the leaves in black and burnishing gold. With the turntable, make a broad line on the wing of the plate, with two other finer lines in black. You can get the pebble effect on the broad line by scraping out little circles using a toothpick or little wooden skewer. The rim of the plate is painted in burnishing gold.

Third firing: touch up the colours and the gold, and paint a sprinkling of small black dots on the maize-coloured background.

Maple leaf

Four firings.

Fill in the maple leaf in water green blue and outline it with gold. Outline the white relief in gold, with little dots. Next, paint the wing of the plate with a blue background, water green, and just a touch of yellow. Finally, add a scattering of gold and black dots and a gold line (add the black spiral line after firing).

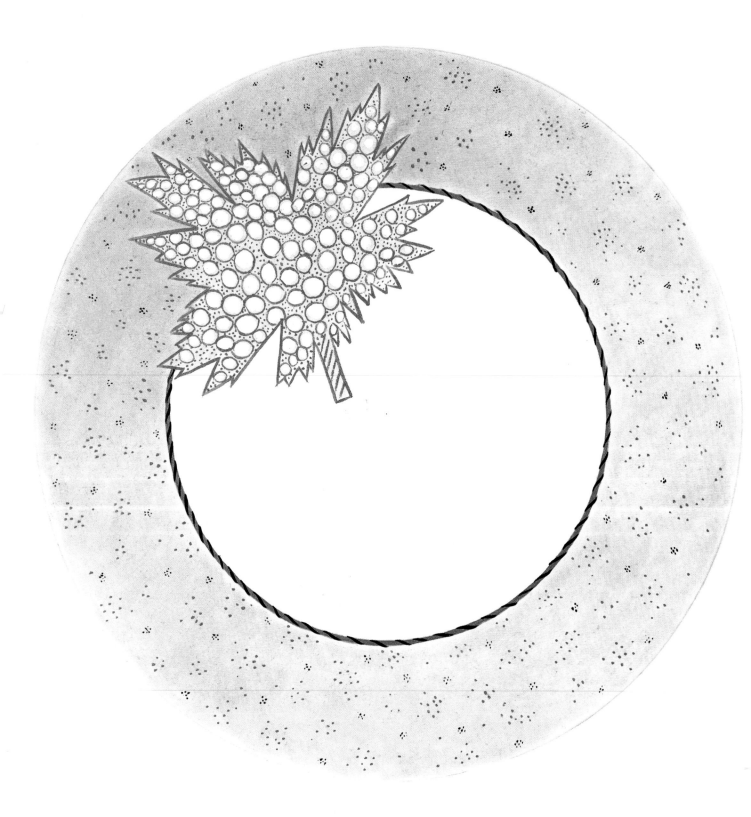

40

Birds and beasts

First firing –
chatironnage.

Second firing –
colouring the bird.

Oriental birds

Two firings.

The colours used in these *chatironné* motifs are fresh and bright. *Chatironné* means that the motifs are outlined with a fine, regular, flowing line of manganese violet.

The following colours are used: rich elderberry (alternatively pink of Cassius or carnation), bright yellow, silver grey, dark blue, chestnut brown, bright green (meadow green), black for outlining (or use violet or manganese violet for this purpose).

First firing: trace the design on to the porcelain or earthenware. Next, using a very fine brush, outline the colours of the bird, the leaves, the tree, and the rocks with black, violet for outlining, or manganese violet (manganese violet can be made by mixing iron red (violet of iron) with elderberry and bitumen brown). The first firing, at about 680 to 700°C (1256 to 1292°F), will fix the colours.

Second firing: paint the birds and their surroundings with a medium brush, as shown in the step-by-step pictures. Then carry out the second firing: at 800°C (1472°F) for porcelain and 720°C (1298°F) for earthenware. For porcelain, a third firing may be necessary.

The finished bird.

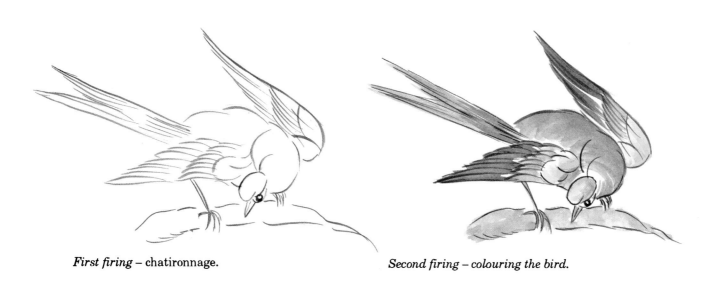

First firing – chatironnage.

Second firing – colouring the bird.

Sketching the flowers.

The finished bird.

First firing: sketching.

Second firing: shading.

The birds of Saint-Clément

Two or three firings.
The floral and bird patterns from Saint-Clément (a factory founded in 1757) are very finely done. They were inspired by examples from Sèvres and look similar to those from Sceaux.

The following colours are used:

Red-headed bird: light golden violet, dark golden violet, light blue, light pink, apple green, nasturtium red, silver yellow, medium brown, dark brown.

Blue-headed bird: nasturtium red, silver yellow, medium blue, dark blue (cornflower blue), light pink, light golden violet, dark golden violet, meadow green, medium brown, dark brown.

First firing: first of all, transfer the design on to the porcelain and sketch the birds with a medium brush. Study the example closely, and move the brush in the direction shown by the arrows. Then paint the foliage, flowers, ground, etc.

Second firing: shade the feathers of the bird with a fine brush. On the nasturtium red, shade in with the same colour. Shade the yellow with medium and dark brown; the light golden violet with dark golden violet; the apple green with medium or dark brown; and the medium blue with cornflower blue.

Then shade the ground, the flowers, the foliage, etc. If necessary, carry out a third firing after touching up.

The finished bird.

Hints

To shade the foliage, mix the brown with apple green.

Paint the mountains very lightly: mix medium blue or light blue with light pink. These two colours blend beautifully.

Pictures of birds in the Saint-Clément style can also be painted in blue monochrome. You can use a kind of Rouen blue which you can make yourself by mixing dark blue (cornflower blue) and light grey.

First firing: sketching.

Second firing: shading.

The finished bird.

45

Two birds, Rouen style

Two firings.
Painted on earthenware (fired at 680 to 720°C (1256 to 1298°F)).

These Rouen birds are in the *rocaille* style, a blend of Far-Eastern and Western taste. *Rocaille* was very fashionable in the reign of Louis XV of France. The style is characterised by fantastic, asymmetrical designs dominated by curves and contorted forms and painted in a very fresh colour scheme.

The following colours are used: meadow green, nasturtium red, bitumen brown, bright yellow, dark blue, manganese violet.

The techniques are similar to those used to paint the oriental birds on pages 42 and 43: the designs are outlined in manganese violet, except for one flower. The flower buds and the crests of the birds are outlined in nasturtium red. The tree trunk is painted in bitumen brown or manganese violet.

The finishing touch is the nasturtium-red highlights on the relief border of the platter.

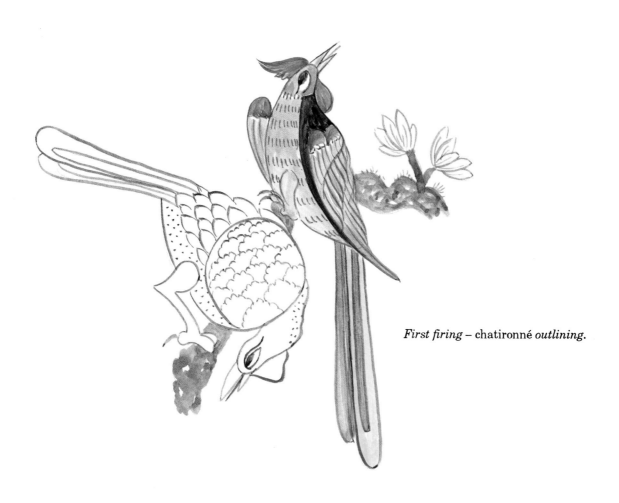

First firing – chatironné *outlining.*

Chimeric bird of Sceaux

Three firings.
Painted on porcelain (fired at 780 to 800°C (1436 to 1472°F)).

The Sceaux pottery was founded around 1748, and part of its production was influenced by Strasbourg (floral bouquets outlined in black). Birds are one of the most successful of Sceaux's earthenware motifs.

The following colours are used:

The bird: apple green, carmine, carnation, light grey, dove grey, silver grey, ivory black, cornflower blue, golden yellow, dark brown.

The ground: pale yellow, golden yellow, sepia, pastel brown, dark brown.

The tree and foliage: apple green, sepia, dark brown.

The background: maize.

First firing: first transfer the motif on to the porcelain or earthenware. Then, with a broad brush, sketch the bird, the ground (with broad brush-strokes), the tree, the foliage, and the rocks. Carry out the first firing.

Second firing: with a fine or medium brush, highlight and shade the bird.

Shade the apple-green part and the neck with ivory black; the carmine wings with carnation; the stomach and wing light grey with silver grey and dove grey; the back cornflower blue with black; the beak and some of the feathers yellow with dark brown; the tree and the foliage with dark brown and apple green; and the trunk with dark brown. Highlight the ground and shade it with dark brown.

Carry out the second firing: pick out some reliefs on the border in dark brown with a fine brush; then, if necessary, touch up the design and do a third firing at 800°C (1472°F).

First firing: sketching.

Second firing: shading in.

Hint

When you are painting large areas, sometimes adding flux to the colours helps fusion while firing and makes the colours brighter and more vivid.

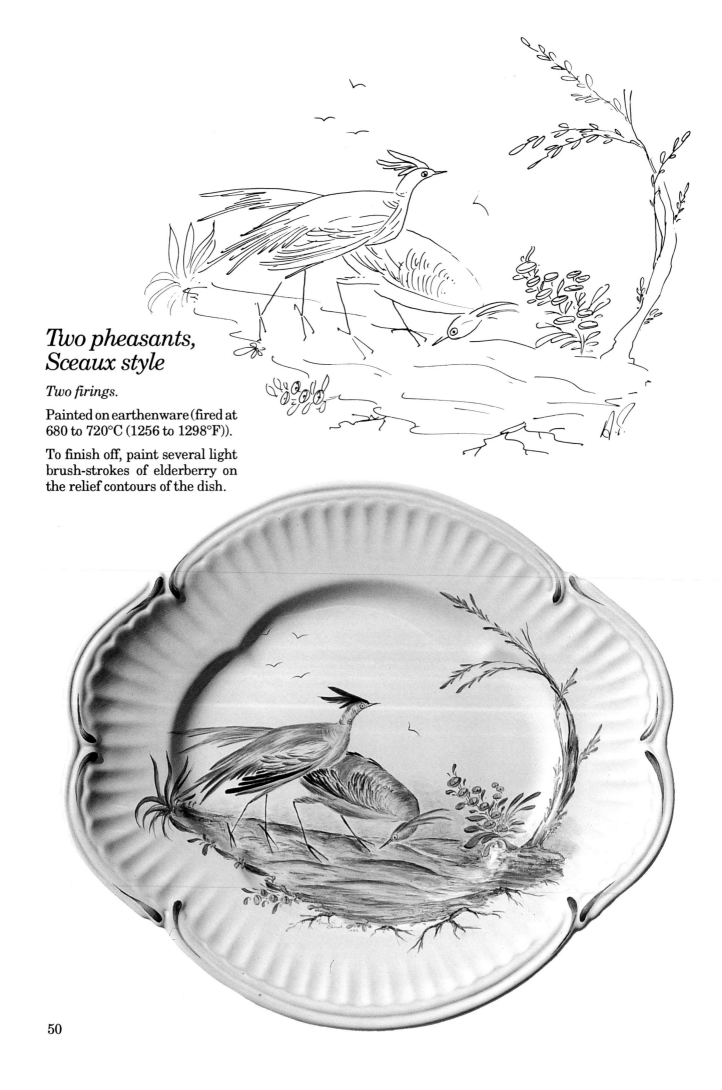

Two pheasants, Sceaux style

Two firings.

Painted on earthenware (fired at 680 to 720°C (1256 to 1298°F)).

To finish off, paint several light brush-strokes of elderberry on the relief contours of the dish.

Owl on a branch, Zürich style

Three firings.

Painted on a shallow porcelain basket with two handles (fired at 800°C (1472°F)). Zürich designs are inspired by the German and French designs of the period (around 1763–90).

The following colours are used:

The owl: light grey, beige grey, dark grey, pale yellow, light maroon (a touch for the stomach), black (mixed with a bit of white to soften it), white.

Bird on the wing: carmine, dark rich purple, nasturtium red, red brown, pale yellow, spring blue, grey, cornflower blue, medium brown, dark brown.

Bird on the ground: nasturtium red, red brown, light maroon, elderberry, medium brown, dark brown.

Landscape: apple green, soft green, golden yellow, maroon, medium brown, dark brown, rose pink.

Finish the basket off with an ornamental border in carmine blue, and add two small flowers (daisies, painted in nasturtium red).

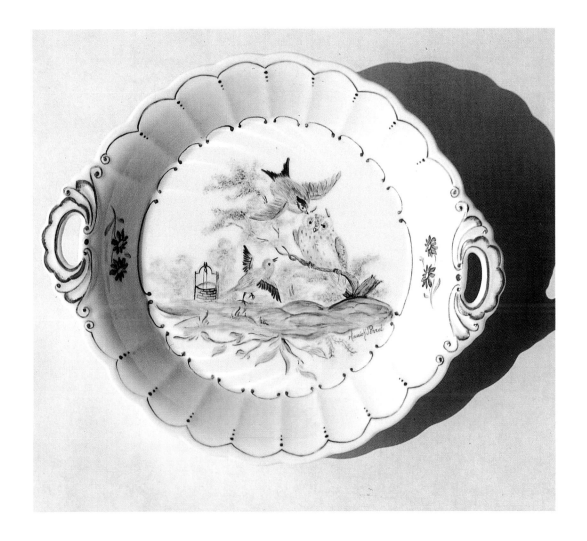

Chinese ducks – famille rose *style*

Two or three firings.

The following colours are used: light pink, carnation, silver yellow, royal blue, apple green, chrome water green, otter brown, beige grey, maroon.

First firing: trace the design on to the porcelain. Next, outline the two ducks using a fine brush and carnation (paint the details of the feathers in maroon). Outline the lotus flowers in carnation, the leaves in maroon, and the water in beige grey and maroon. The lotus stems are apple green with little maroon dots.

Second firing: sketch the ducks using water green, rose pink, beige grey, silver yellow, royal blue and a little otter brown.

Then paint the lotus leaves in otter brown, and the water in chrome water green. If necessary, carry out a third firing after any touching up you may need to do.

Siskin and Christmas garland

Three firings.

Painted on earthenware (fired at 680 to 720°C (1256 to 1298°F)).

A *tisanière*, or teapot, consists of a pot for the herbal tea (*tisane*), an oil lamp for heating it, and a stand to put it on. Around the second half of the eighteenth century, the oil lamps were transformed into night-lights. They gave out a bit of light at night through their cylindrical body with holes in, and also kept herbal tea or soup warm. These charming porcelain and earthenware objects have become collectors' pieces and are sought out fervently by enthusiasts!

The following colours are used (choose autumnal tints): grey, green grey, brown green, otter brown, dark brown, black green, iron red, yellow, violet of iron, rose pink, fir-tree green. The background is in light brown green.

First firing: on the teapot stand, paint a garland of mistletoe leaves and berries, holly, and sprigs of fir; also a few pine cones around the two Christmas roses. On the teapot, paint a wren on one side and a siskin on the other. The lid is decorated with a garland of holly and mistletoe.

Second firing: paint the backgrounds in light brown-green, then a pale background around the garland and the birds to give depth to the design. For the handle and the spout, paint a background on the lower half, with a garland of pine branches dividing the coloured part from the white part.

Third firing: shade in the garland and the birds.

54

Butterfly on marbled red background

Four firings.

First firing: outline the butterfly and the flowers in black.

Second firing: paint mother-of pearl lustre within the outlines of the butterflies and flowers.

Third firing: create a marbled background in red and dark grey, and add white relief on the butterfly's wings.

Fourth firing: touch up the black where needed, and apply burnishing gold.

Put some dots of white relief in the centres of the flowers. After firing, add gold dots to the white relief. For details of how to marble the colour, see the section on techniques.

Mother hen and chicks

Three firings.

The three chicks are painted with the following colours: silver yellow, ivory yellow, brown yellow, chestnut brown, nasturtium red, black, and violet of iron.

For the flowers, use mauve and golden violet, and for their centres dark brown. Paint the foliage using apple green and ivy green.

For the base of the egg, fill in the background with silver yellow and spring blue, which will give a subtle, varied effect (yellow, green and blue). Then paint the black garland.

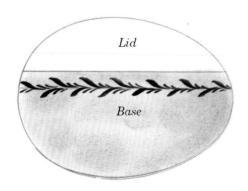

Chinese butterfly

Four firings.

Paint the butterfly and the flowers using nasturtium red and a little black.

For the background:

First firing: fill in with grey lustre.

Second firing: make lines and small dots on the lustre with a pen or a fine brush.

Chinese goldfish

Four firings.

First firing: for the lid, outline the fish in burnishing gold, black, and nasturtium red.

Second firing: fill in the background using orangey lustre with nasturtium-red and gold patterns. The scales of the fish are gold.

Third firing: fill in with nasturtium red on the lustre, and scrape out the little circles with a toothpick.

Fourth firing: finishing, touching up, and black-and-red patterns where needed.

Paint the base of the egg in burnishing gold with some nasturtium-red texturing.

Chinese fish

Three to four firings.

Painted on porcelain (fired at 780°C (1436°F))

First firing: trace the shape of the Chinese fish and the scales with a pen or a fine outlining brush and grey paint. Add a few details.

Second firing: fill in the background and accentuate the scales with large dots.

For the little fish, prepare red and grey, a mixture of blue and maroon, and maroon. Paint in a few small lotus flowers (the lotus flower is a symbol of purity) and some greenery. The border is nasturtium red with gold latticing (fire at about 680°C (1256°F)). The thin lines are also gold.

Upper fish: draw the shape of the fish, its scales and the background in grey.
The lotus: rose pink.
The tail and fins: nasturtium red.
The lower left-hand fish is in rose pink monochrome.

Lower right-hand fish: paint the shape of the fish, the background, and the scales in blue.
The fins and the tail: rose pink.

58

Dragons and phoenix

Three to four firings.

Painted on a porcelain teapot – the largest one in my entire collection.

The following colours are used: nasturtium red, emerald green, and 32 per cent burnishing gold.

First firing: draw the shapes of the dragons and the phoenix with a pen, in emerald green. The waves (at the top of the teapot stand) are symbols of peace, and are done in green and red.

Second firing: work with a small brush and fill in with light and dark emerald green.

Third firing: paint the details and the gold scales on the phoenix and the dragons with a fine brush. The small clouds are painted in nasturtium red, and the frieze, a symbol of good fortune, is in gold.

The reverse side of the teapot.

Insects and flower sprigs

Four firings.

Painted on porcelain (fired at 780 to 800° (1436 to 1472°F)).

The following colours are used: light grey (for the sections that have a background), 32 per cent burnishing gold (for the gold bands), black, water green, silver yellow, nasturtium red, yellow brown, apple green, rose pink, spring blue, cornflower blue, pale yellow, dark brown, violet of iron, black green, soft green.

First firing: draw and paint butterflies and bugs of different sizes and a scattering of little sprigs of flowers (forget-me-nots, rosebuds, scarlet pimpernels, etc.).

Second firing: paint broad bands of light grey on parts of the teapot and its stand.

Third firing: shade the butterflies and flowers, draw the gold bands, and then add a few more little flowers dotted about here and there.

Fourth firing: touch up the gold. Outline the butterflies with nasturtium red; paint their bodies in black and dark brown, and their wings in silver yellow with nasturtium-red dots and black veins. Shade the yellow wings with brown and add two red and black ladybirds to the teapot lid.

People

Composition with three faces

The wing of this plate has four different backgrounds and patterns. The colours in the composition are outlined in burnishing gold.

Bowl of the plate

Use burnishing gold, nasturtium red, cornflower blue, and light blue.

Wing of the plate (left half)

The main colour of the background is nasturtium red. After firing, paint the patterns in gold and small dark red dots.

Wing of the plate (right half)

Paint the background in 32 per cent burnishing gold (spread on evenly). After firing, paint the patterns in nasturtium red or iron red.

Reflection

Four firings.

Wing of the plate

First firing: fill in with a background of maize.

Second firing: paint the finer parts in yellow brown, using a brush; on the left half of the plate, outline the finer yellow-brown parts in dark brown. There are two gold lines – one broad, one fine.

Bowl of the plate

Outline the design in burnishing gold. The background is brown, slightly speckled and with gold dots.

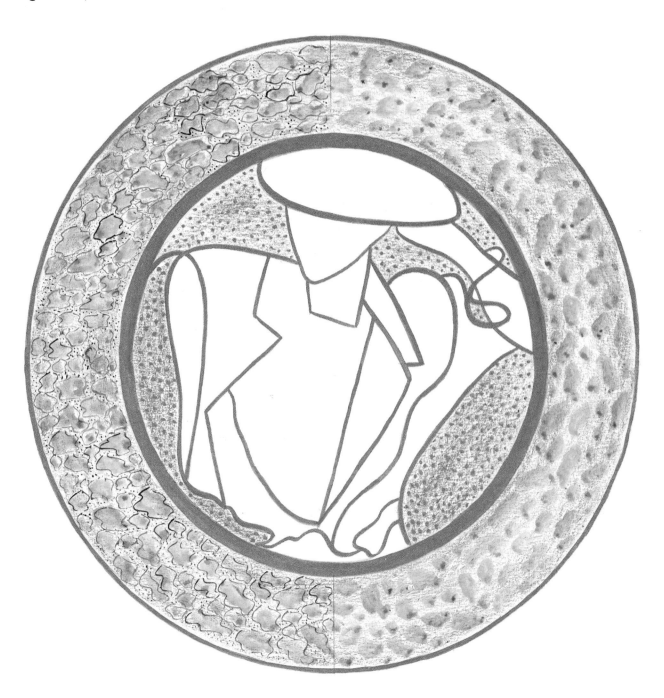

The fashionable woman

Six firings.

I designed this plaque in the Cubist style.

The studied textures are inspired by the fabrics: see the test pattern (left).

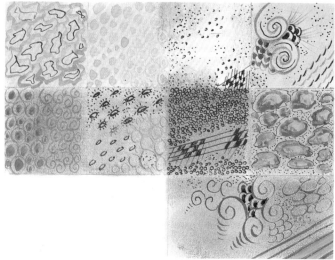

Trying out different colours and patterns.

The woman in a hat

Five firings.

Haute couture was the inspiration for the plaque 'The woman in a hat'.

'Playing cards'

Six firings.

I made this large oval dish for the 16th National Exhibition of Work in Paris, in 1982.

To decorate the border of the oval dish, which has slightly irregularly shaped wings, I gave it an scroll-like wrought-iron motif. For the inside of the dish, I created a pattern which is a study of design, colour and patterns.

The dish needed six firings at different temperatures. I used the following colours: light grey, nasturtium red, dark grey, black, silver yellow, and cornflower blue.

I made the wrought-iron-style frieze in black and red so that it would go with the composition 'Playing cards – queen and king of hearts' that I designed for the inside of the dish.

Trying out colours and patterns.

Woman and butterflies

Six firings.

Painted on a porcelain plaque – a study of composition, colour and texture. This idea resulted in my creating two pieces: the round plaque below and the picture of which you can see a detail on the opposite page.

See also the test patterns (right), where I have tried out a range of colours and designs for the picture on the opposite page.

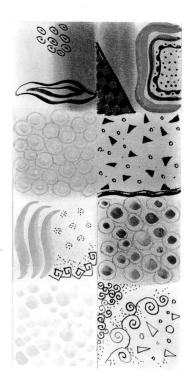

For the first firing, brush iridescent lustre over the whole surface of the plaque to give a moiré effect. (After this first firing you can get on with the painting.)

The following colours are used: black, nasturtium red (for some of the butterfly wings), light and dark rose pink, otter brown, brown yellow, pale yellow, yellow relief, 32 per cent burnishing gold, and light and dark golden violet.

Wing of the plate

First firing: the background is Rouen blue, or a mixture of grey and cornflower blue.

Second firing: with a brush, add a touch of Rouen blue; and lines in burnishing gold.

Bowl of the plate

Paint the face in blue monochrome and put imaginary butterflies round it (in rose pink, blue, Parma violet, yellow and gold).

Mother and child

(see page 72)

This is another plaque on which I have explored the use of textures and patterns.

70

Création Annick Perret 1986

Religious themes

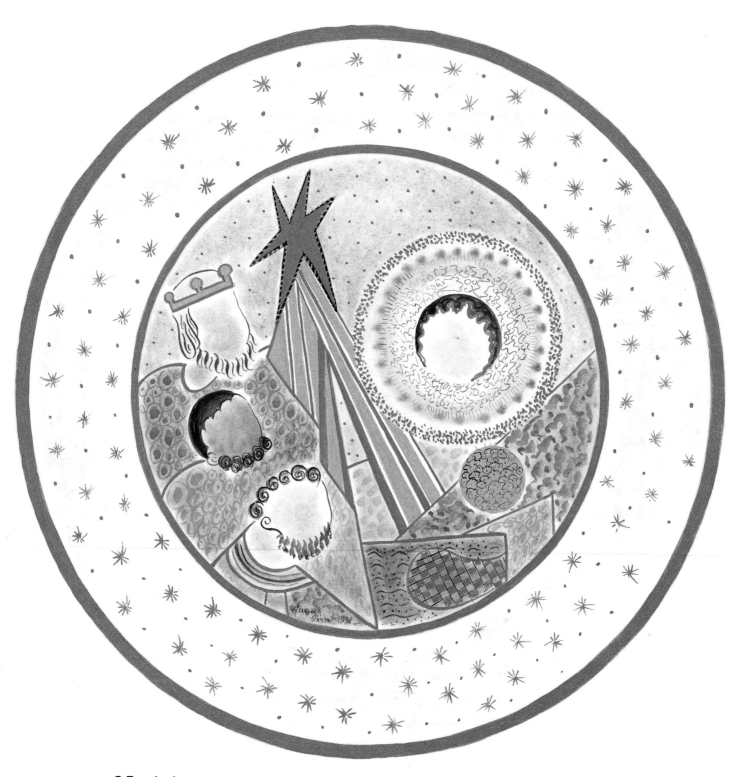

Nativity scene

Two firings.

Wing of the plate

First firing: fill in the background with very pale rose pink.

Second firing: add dots and little stars in gold. The lines are done with a turntable using burnishing gold.

Bowl of the plate

Use blue, rose pink, turquoise and yellow, then add burnishing gold and matt platinum. Go round the outlines of the drawing with burnishing gold.

The Three Kings

This is a variation of the plate on page 74, a study in pattern and colour on a Christmas theme.

The Magi

Six to seven firings.

Painted on a porcelain plaque – another study of colours and textures.

The following colours are used: light and dark rose pink, light and dark golden violet, pale blue, light and dark grey, pale yellow, maize yellow, light apple green, Rouen blue, black, and 32 per cent burnishing gold.

Magus on platinum background (right)

Five firings.
Painted on a porcelain plate.

The following colours are used: matt platinum, burnishing gold, nasturtium red, spring blue, yellow, and black.

First firing: using a pen, draw the Magus very finely in black in the centre of the plate. The surrounding pattern, which looks like pebbles, is done in red.

Second firing: paint the Magus.

Third firing: fill in the background with matt platinum and paint the cloak using burnishing gold.

Fourth firing: draw patterns on the platinum background and touch up the gold.

Fifth firing: strengthen all the colours.

The crown: silver yellow.
The face: very diluted red; black eyes.
Beard outlined in black – the rest in gold.
The whole composition is outlined in black.

Caspar, Melchior and Balthasar

Four firings.

Painted on a porcelain *tisanière*/teapot – a stylised representation of the Three Kings: Caspar, Melchior and Balthasar.

The monogram is painted in black, while the background of the body of the teapot and the base is painted in a very pale shade of Rouen blue. Paint the top and bottom of the base and the lid of the teapot a slightly darker shade of the same colour, and add a pebbled pattern. Finish off with burnishing gold and add slim bands of Rouen blue.

Madonna and Child

Four firings.

Painted on porcelain – a round medallion inspired by mediaeval paintings.

Make the gold background as follows:

First firing: reliefs for the gold.

Second firing: 32 per cent burnishing gold.

Third firing: paint small stylised daisies in nasturtium red and add a scattering of black dots with a pen.

Madonna on a gold background

Four firings.

This egg was inspired by icons. The colours used are light and medium pink, black, white relief, and 32 per cent burnishing gold.

For the border of the egg and the base, use cobalt or royal blue, and for the background, burnishing gold.

First firing: outline the shape of the Madonna in black with a fine brush.

Second firing: fill in the robe in light pink; the face and hands in very pale violet of iron; and the background in burnishing gold.

Third firing: apply a second coat of gold to the background. The fine texturing on the robe is done in medium pink.

Fourth firing: use a pen for drawing in the black patterns on the gold background, and add some white relief dots to the black rim of the halo.

Church at Féchy

Five firings.

This oval porcelain medallion was inspired by the church in the village of Féchy in the canton of Vaud, Switzerland.

The rim is done with 32 per cent burnishing gold on a black background. For the background (the sky), I have made a speckled effect in blue grey and light maroon. The houses and church are painted in rose pink and Rouen blue mixed, Rouen blue, nasturtium red, and black, with large dots of burnishing gold painted on a black background for one of the houses.

Stylised designs

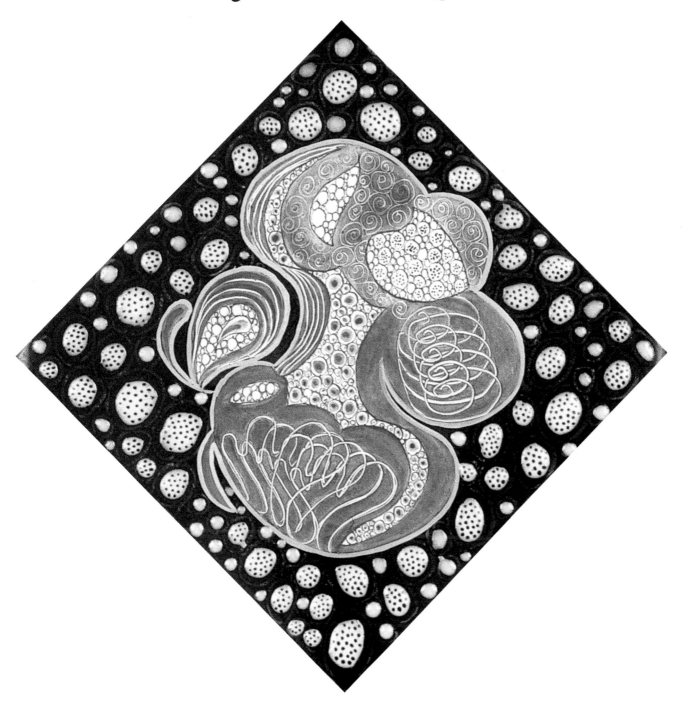

The three horses

Four firings.

This design could be the inspiration for a plate or box.

The following colours are used: pale maize, brown, blue (light and dark), Parma violet, golden violet, turquoise, chrome water green, black, and 32 per cent burnishing gold.

The background is painted in pale maize and the speckling is done in brown and turquoise, while the horses are painted in light and dark blue and their manes, tails, and reins outlined in gold.

Bouquet of poppies *(right)*

Five firings.

The following colours are used: light and dark Rouen blue, light and dark golden violet, black, yellow, light and dark red, and burnishing gold.

Divide the plate up into unequal segments and draw the poppy. Paint the different segments of the background in light red, light Rouen blue, and yellow, decorated with a few gold dots surrounded by black sunbursts.

The Persian cavalier

Five firings.

This design might be suitable for a plate or a round container; it is a study in colours, mother-of pearl lustre, and textures.

The following colours are used: light and dark grey, light and dark nasturtium red, black, light brown, blue, rose pink, and burnishing gold (there is also some outlining in gold).

Japanese face (right)

Five firings.

This large porcelain plaque is my own interpretation of a Japanese print, with a spontaneously uncoiling line.

The background texture is created by brushing over and speckling colour (a study of the texture of lace). Chrome water green blue, golden Parma violet, and black are used.

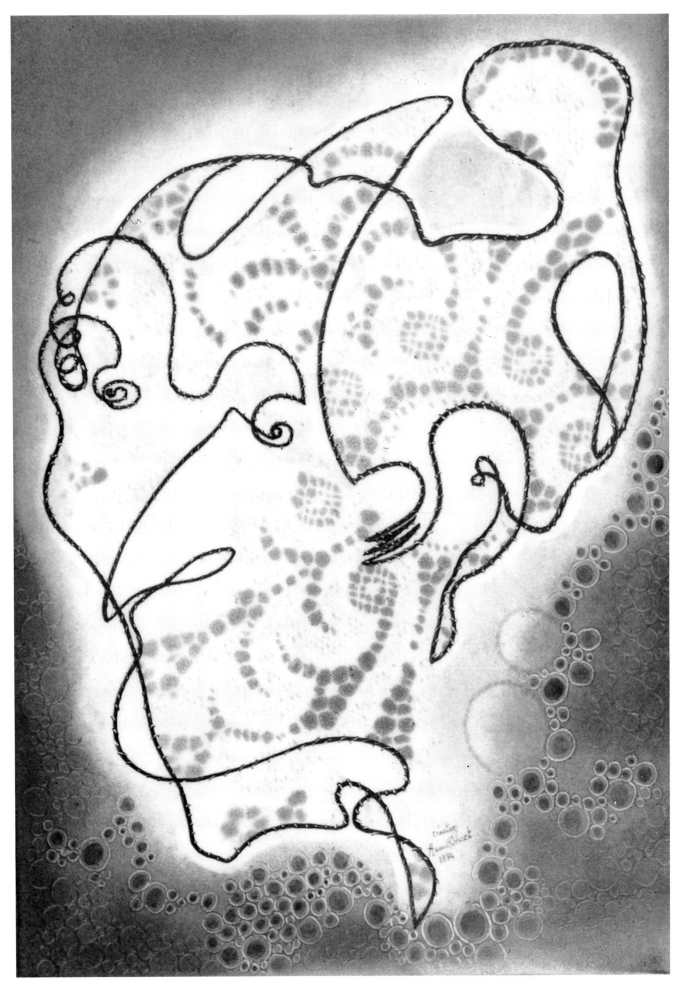

Flower petals

Five firings.

This plaque is a study of a flower-petal design.

The petals are transformed into a textured shape of red outlined in gold; the background is black with white reliefs, some of which are decorated with small black dots. Iridescent lustre is used in the petals, and the shape is outlined in 32 per cent burnishing gold.

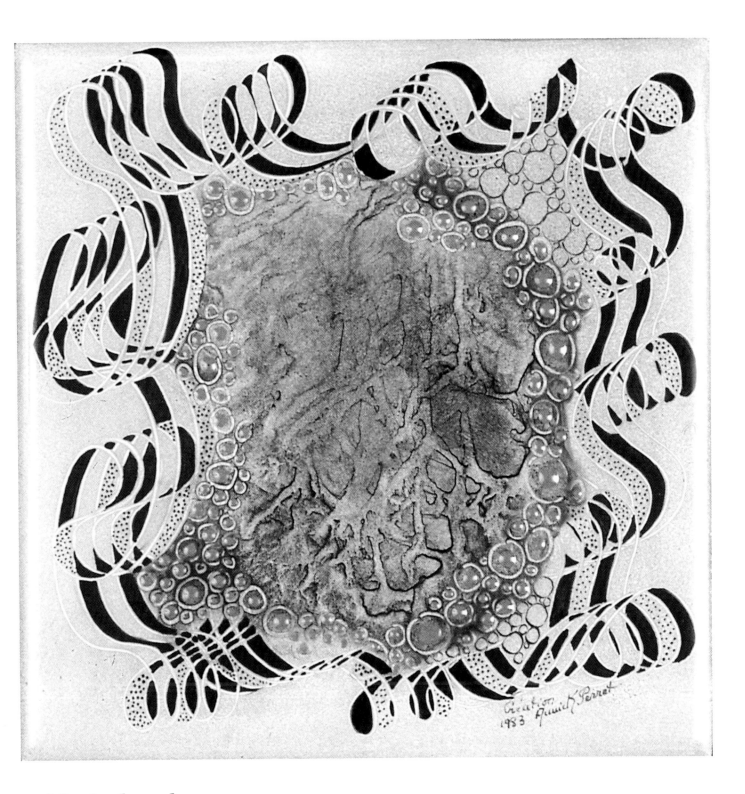

Musical study

Five firings.

This composition was inspired by listening to music. I have used diluted colours and pink reliefs, and the border is a ribbon made with a comb, on a grey background.

creation
Yannick Perret
1989

88

Fiery opal (left)

Six firings.

Here I have played with letters of the alphabet to create a jumble of overlapping and merging shapes. The colours, precious metals, and patterns fit into these shapes.

The following colours are used: nasturtium red, light grey, black, and blue grey (for the background). Platinum and two coats of burnishing gold are also used: burnish the gold with an agate burnishing tool.

Turquoise

Five firings.

The following colours are used: turquoise, nasturtium red, black; also burnishing gold and matt platinum.

The background is painted in very pale blue grey, and the abstract design is outlined in nasturtium red using a fine brush. Patterns are painted on the gold and platinum in red or black.

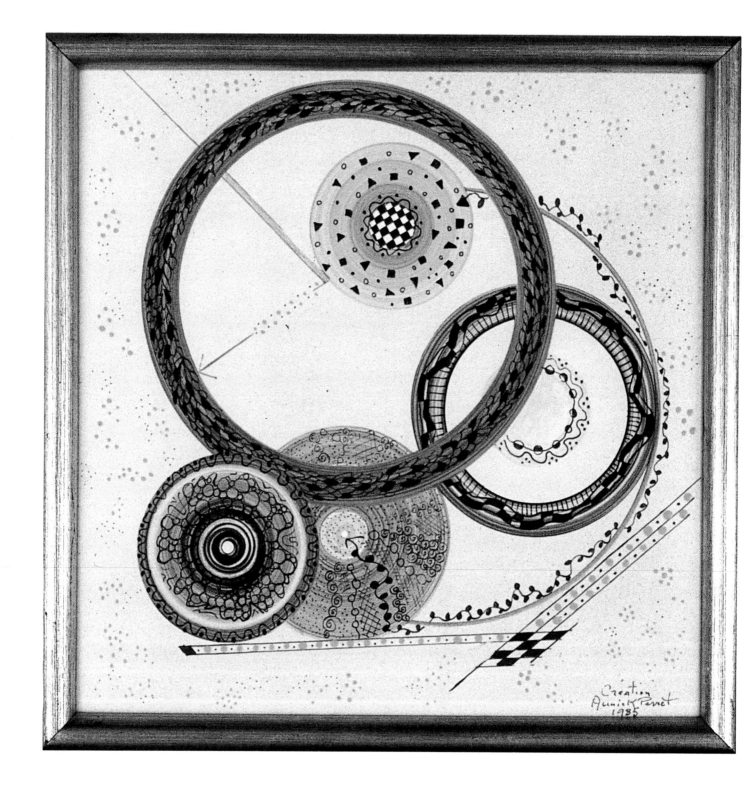

Circles with turquoise pearls

Five firings.

This plaque is a study of a circular design made with a turntable – a design that might suit an ashtray, for example.

The circles are filled in with pattern-work. The little chess-board at the centre of one of the circles is painted in black and iridescent lustre; the background is painted in pale celadon, strewn with small turquoise pearls (with turquoise relief).

Iridescent circle (right)

Five firings.

The tableau on the right is a real compendium of shapes and textures (it is a study of a linear design where the lines turn into shapes). Five firings are needed for this large porcelain plaque. The following colours are used: blue, yellow, green, black, maroon (a mixture of colours superimposed one on another), and burnishing gold.

The iridescent circle with the black outline is done using a turntable.

Polychromatic patterns with gold

Four firings.

First firing: the background is done using a turntable. The following colours are used: salmon pink, rose pink, pale blue, cornflower blue, apple green, and a mixture of rose pink and blue.

Second firing: apply various patterns in maroon and grey blue.

Third firing: enhance the patterns and add some more.

Fourth firing: add a sprinkling of gold dots.

Golden ribbon and patterns

Five firings.

This study in patterns is painted in pale blue, cornflower blue, light pink, and black. The background is kept very pale, in pink and blue, and the patterns are painted on with a small, fine-pointed brush in cornflower blue, pink and black.

The ribbon is painted in 32 per cent burnishing gold (two coats).

Camaieu in Rouen blue and gold

Three firings.

The background is made up of broad bands done using a turntable. I used a square-ended brush for this and kept my paint a bit more liquid than normal.

The lines are done using a turntable and Rouen blue. The pebbled patterns are created in blue with a pen, and the large dots inside the pebbles are done in burnishing gold.

Finally, add a scattering of small dots in Rouen blue.

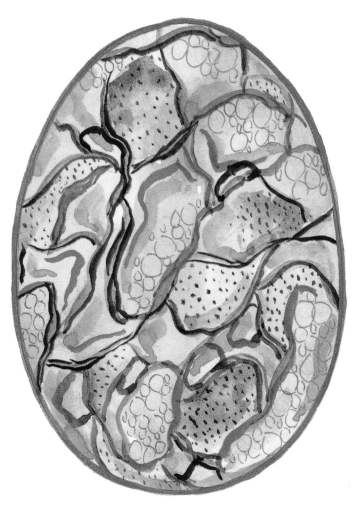

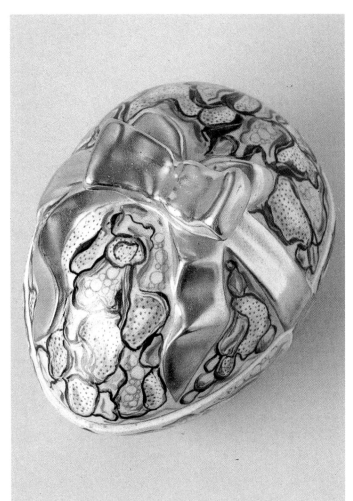

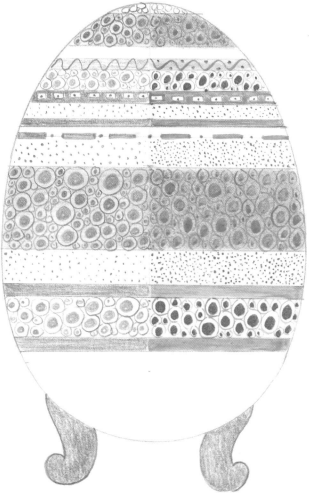

Glossary

Biscuit

Biscuit porcelain is made with fine-quality paste giving the appearance of white metal in the workpiece. Biscuit is not coated with glaze.

Bowl

The means the inside of a dish or plate.

Camaieu

Camaieu (monochrome) designs are done in a range of shades of the same colour.

***Chatironné* patterns**

Floral patterns with a thin black or manganese violet outline round them.

China

K'ien-long period, 1736-1795

K'ien-long, the fourth emperor of the Manchurian dynasty, was a patron of the arts, and had some excellent porcelain produced in the *famille rose* style (mainly pink). Flowers – lotus, peonies, chrysanthemums, etc. – were always the main source of inspiration, but birds, ducks, butterflies and fish were also painted with scrupulous attention to detail, along conventional lines.

Colours

These are metal oxide colourings which, when mixed with flux, adhere to the porcelain glaze.

Cobalt oxide is always used in blue colours.

Chromium oxide and copper oxide provide green colours.

Antimony oxide and lead chromate produce yellow colours.

Red colours are obtained with copper monoxide and iron sesquioxide, which gives a great variety of nuances of colour.

Violet and pink colours come from a fine mixture of gold and tin oxide.

Blacks are made with uranium monoxide or mixtures of cobalt oxide and manganese.

Earthenware

For making traditional earthenware with opaque glaze, the paste is formed of clay (it is generally ready-mixed) to which sand can be added. After washing and firing for the first time, it is very pale in colour. A tin-based glaze is made fast by a second firing. After applying the pattern and the colours, a third firing fuses the colours into the glaze. Earthenware fabrication in Eastern Europe dates from the beginning of the fifteenth century.

Flux

A mixture of silicaceous sand. Flux helps colouring matter to adhere and makes up the glaze.

Kaolin

White clay used for porcelain paste. The first deposits were discovered in China at Kao-ling, from which we get the English name. Similar deposits were discovered in France at St-Yrieux, near Limoges, in 1767.

Muffle kiln

Kiln for soft-firing of porcelain.

Naturalistic patterns

Floral patterns made up of fine hatchings and graduations of colour to bring out the relief.

Polychromatic

Patterns with several colours.

***Rocaille* patterns**

These were at the height of their popularity in ceramics around 1750–1775. *Rocaille* patterns are most often used as a border with patterns of birds and flowers.

Rouen

This factory was founded in 1644 and produced first the 'Chinese' style and later the *rocaille* style (around 1720).

The vivid colours give Rouen work a very decorative character. The variety and quality of the radiant (*rayonnant*) patterns from Rouen are truly exceptional. These *rayonnant*-style patterns, often set off with reds and yellows, are from the first half of the eighteenth century. Polychromatic and *rocaille* patterns arrived slightly later on.

Saint-Clément

The Saint-Clément factory was founded in 1757. The floral and bird patterns from Saint-Clément are very finely done; they were inspired by examples from Sèvres and similar to those from Sceaux.

Sceaux

A pottery founded around 1748. Part of the Sceaux production was influenced by Strasbourg (floral bouquets outlined in black).

Sceaux employed painters of flowers, fruits and birds, and birds are one of the most successful of Sceaux's earthenware motifs.

Sinceny

Founded in 1733. Several noted ceramic painters from Rouen set up in Sinceny. The designs were drawn from Japan, China (*famille verte*, or *famille rose* from the K'ien-long era), Rouen, Strasbourg, and Sèvres.

Soft-firing patterns

These patterns are applied on fired glaze.

Strasbourg

A 'soft-firing' technique similar to that used in Meissen around 1749.

1767–1770 were the peak years of naturalistic *qualité fine* painting. Floral patterns were painted with delicate brushwork after the style of Dresden china, which inspired them.

Ornamental bouquets in the Strasbourg *fleur fine* style are dominated by a clear, vigorous palette of colours and a striking variety of pinks and maroons. With this technique, called 'soft-firing' or 'muffle-firing', the pattern is painted on glaze which has already been fired.

In the finest-quality *fleurs fines*, all trace of outline (*chatironné* pattern) disappears. Petals on the flowers are made up of fine shaded hatchings which follow the contours of the petals. The coats of paint have to fuse into one another. Glowing light and dark purply-pink colours dominate the bouquets. The green of the leaves is applied in one or two hues and is shaded. With the brush, the painting of the leaves is done from the centre outwards to the edges, and in this way it is possible to achieve a serrated edge (for rose leaves).

The shading of the foliage is done with a mixture of elderberry and green, or rusty maroon and a green and black mix, or even brown and green. The process, which begins with thin coats of light colours, is the same for all bouquets. After the first firing, the colours in the second coat are not always the same as those in the first coat: they are often stronger.

Wing of a dish

This refers to the flat rim of a dish or plate.

Zürich

There was a porcelain factory at Schooren-Bendlikon (1763–90), said to have been founded by a painter from Höchst. The designs are inspired by the German and French designs of the period.

Index